DISNEP
LEARNING

THE
BIG BOOK
OF
DISNEP
TOP 10s
FUN FACTS AND
COOL TRIVIA

LERNER PUBLICATIONS ◆ MINNEAPOLIS

TABLE OF CONTENTS

TONS OF TOP 10S

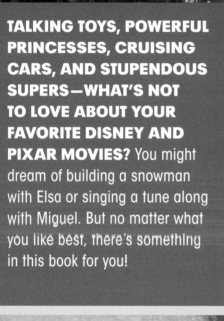

TALKING TOYS, POWERFUL PRINCESSES, CRUISING CARS, AND STUPENDOUS SUPERS—WHAT'S NOT TO LOVE ABOUT YOUR FAVORITE DISNEY AND PIXAR MOVIES? You might dream of building a snowman with Elsa or singing a tune along with Miguel. But no matter what you like best, there's something in this book for you!

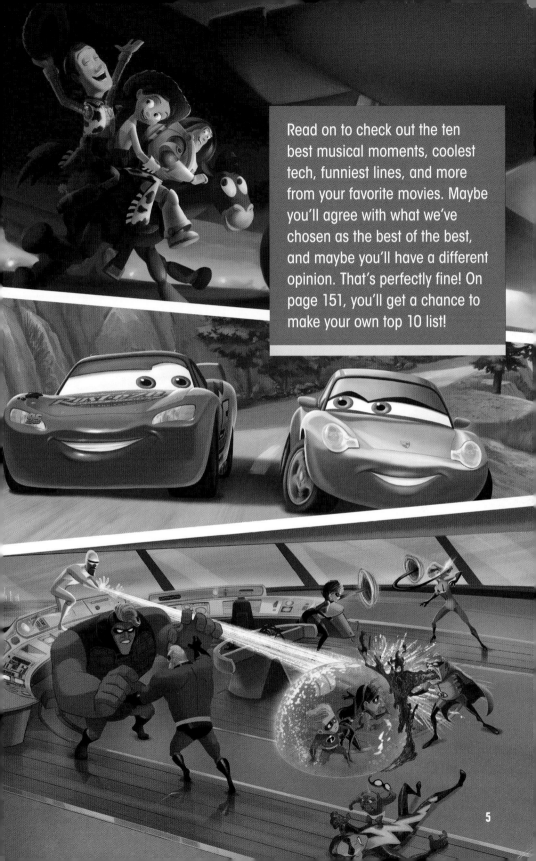

Read on to check out the ten best musical moments, coolest tech, funniest lines, and more from your favorite movies. Maybe you'll agree with what we've chosen as the best of the best, and maybe you'll have a different opinion. That's perfectly fine! On page 151, you'll get a chance to make your own top 10 list!

MR. INCREDIBLE'S TOP 10 INCREDIBLE MOMENTS

10 He breaks the rules to help the old woman with her insurance claim.

9 He rescues people from a burning building.

HE AND FROZONE MAKE IT LOOK EASY.

8 He breaks into the Tunneler to try to catch the Underminer.

7 He discovers the Omnidroid's weakness.

THE ONLY THING THAT CAN DAMAGE IT IS ITSELF.

6 He uses a train yard as an exercise gym.

 **5** He works underwater to turn a ship.

HE MUST HAVE SUPER LUNGS TO HOLD HIS BREATH THAT LONG!

3 After an all-night study session, he finally figures out Dash's math homework.

2 He apologizes to Violet for not knowing how to help her with her crush.

HEY, SUPER DADS AREN'T PERFECT!

4 He supports his wife's career by taking care of the kids.

"I'VE GOT TO SUCCEED, SO SHE CAN SUCCEED. SO WE CAN SUCCEED."

 1 HE REALIZES HIS FAMILY MUST WORK TOGETHER TO DEFEAT SYNDROME.

TOP 10 FEATURES OF THE INCREDIBLES' SUPERSUITS

 10 Bulletproof material helps when you're battling bad guys.

 9 It has a homing device.

GOOD IF YOU'VE BEEN CAPTURED. BAD IF YOU'RE SNEAKING AROUND A VILLAIN'S BASE.

8 It helps control Jack-Jack's morphing powers.

7 It's indestructible.

NOT EVEN A GARBAGE DISPOSAL CAN DESTROY IT.

6

It's made from a blend of high-tech materials and cotton.

THE COTTON IS FOR COMFORT.

5

It comes with a mask.

A SUPER'S SECRET IDENTITY IS THEIR MOST VALUABLE POSSESSION.

4

It protects from temps up to one thousand degrees.

3

It adapts to a Super's powers. Violet's Supersuit turns invisible. Elastigirl's stretches to match her shape.

2

Jack-Jack's new Supersuit has a fire extinguisher included.

BLACKBERRY-LAVENDER-FLAVORED FOAM, YUM!

1

IT'S MACHINE WASHABLE. CRIME FIGHTING IS A DIRTY JOB, AND SO IS LAUNDRY!

ELASTIGIRL'S TOP 10 INCREDIBLE MOMENTS

10 She uses her fighter-pilot skills to shake off incoming missiles.

9 She stretches to keep everyone in place at the dinner table.

8 When her leg gets stuck in a door, she stretches across two hallways and into a room to get the door's key.

SHE'S AS DETERMINED AS SHE IS FLEXIBLE!

7 She becomes a parachute to stop the runaway MetroLev train.

6

She drives the Elasticycle for the first time.

WHO KNEW THE HOUSE HAD A SECRET EXIT?

5

She flattens as thin as paper so she doesn't get squished by a train on Syndrome's island.

4

She changes her Elastigirl suit for an Incredibles suit.

THIS FAMILY WORKS BEST AS A TEAM!

3

When Syndrome kidnaps Jack-Jack, she has Mr. Incredible throw her into the air.

2

She discovers the Screenslaver's secret technology, the hypno-goggles.

TOO BAD THE SCREENSLAVER WAS NEXT TO HER WHEN SHE DID.

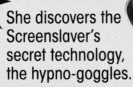

1

SHE SAVES EVERYONE IN THE CRASHING HELICOPTERS.

TOP 10
INCREDIBLES TECH

10

The Omnidroids learned how to battle Supers so well that one even figured out how to stop Syndrome.

THAT WAS DEFINITELY NOT PART OF SYNDROME'S EVIL PLAN.

9 The Tunneler helps the Underminer travel underground.

8 Syndrome's immobi-ray can stop people in their tracks and lift them off the ground.

7 With their spinning blades, you wouldn't want to get too close to a Velocipod.

BUT IT WOULD BE LOTS OF FUN TO FLY!

^^^^^
DID YOU KNOW?

The Incredibles movies have scenes with water, clouds, smoke, and fire. To make the scenes realistic, the animators studied fluid dynamics. That's the science behind how these things move.

6 Elastigirl's Elasticycle gets her into the action quickly.

5 Not only does the Manta Jet fly, but it can also dive into water and transform into an underwater vehicle.

4 Hypno-goggles have the power to control people.

THANK GOODNESS THEY WERE DESTROYED!

3 Frozone's ice equipment transforms into skates, skis, and an ice disc whenever he needs it.

1

2 Edna's Jack-Jack monitor is pure genius.

THE CALMING OPTION IS A GAME CHANGER!

ROCKET THRUSTERS, AUTO-DRIVE, EJECTOR SEATS, A REMOTE CONTROL . . . THE INCREDIBILE HAS IT ALL!

VIOLET'S TOP 10 INCREDIBLE MOMENTS

10 She turns invisible when she sees Tony.

ARE YOU STILL BLUSHING IF NO ONE CAN SEE YOU?

9 She accepts her dad's apology and tries to take care of him.

8 She calls Lucius when her dad is overwhelmed.

JACK-JACK IS A HANDFUL!

7 She protects everyone in the Tunneler before it explodes.

6

She questions her parents when they contradict themselves.

GROWING UP CAN BE CONFUSING.

5

She uses *renounce* correctly in a sentence.

4

She creates a large force field for her and Dash to roll through the jungle.

JUST LIKE A HUGE HAMSTER BALL!

3 She fights off Voyd's attacks.

2

She meets Monster Jack-Jack.

SURPRISE!

1

«

SHE RELEASES HER FAMILY FROM SYNDROME'S PRISON WHILE HER DAD IS MONOLOGUING.

TOP 10 INCREDIBLE LINES

10 "Done properly, parenthood is a heroic act." —Edna

9 "No matter how many times you save the world, it always manages to get back in jeopardy again."

MR. INCREDIBLE'S STRUGGLE NEVER ENDS, KIND OF LIKE MAKING YOUR BED.

8 "I know what I *said*! Listen to what I'm saying now."

IT'S OKAY FOR A MOM TO CHANGE HER MIND.

7 "The only normal one is Jack-Jack and he's not even toilet trained." —Violet

6

"Is she having adolescence?"

DASH JUST CAN'T FIGURE OUT VIOLET.

^ ^ ^ ^ ^
DID YOU KNOW?

Elastigirl uses real military flight terms when flying the jet to Syndrome's island.

5

"I'm used to knowing what the right thing to do is, but now I'm not sure anymore. I just want to be a good dad." —Mr. Incredible

4

"Where is my Supersuit?" —Frozone

3

"Why would they change math? Math is math!"

HAVE PATIENCE, MR. INCREDIBLE!

⟶≫

2

"You know it's crazy, right? To help my family I gotta leave it; to fix the law, I gotta break it." —Elastigirl

1

WE ALL KNOW THIS ONE: "NO CAPES!" —EDNA

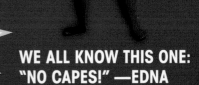

DASH'S TOP 10 INCREDIBLE MOMENTS

10 He saves Violet from the fireball in the cave.

9 When his mom shuts her bedroom door, he's immediately outside looking in the window.

8 He uses his fast kicks to power a boat.

ACTUALLY, HIS MOM WAS THE BOAT.

7 He finishes and understands his math homework.

6 He brings his dad back onto the ship just in time.

MR. INCREDIBLE TRUSTS DASH WITH HIS LIFE.

∧ ∧ ∧ ∧ ∧
DID YOU KNOW?
Dash can run about 200 miles per hour. That's as fast as a race car!

 5 He discovers the Incredibile's voice command.

4 He's okay with coming in second place at his track meet.

HE'LL DO WHATEVER IT TAKES TO KEEP HIS FAMILY'S SECRET!

 3 He outruns the Velocipods in the jungle.

 2 He saves his siblings when he uses the Incredibile remote to escape.

1 HE RUNS ACROSS WATER. EVEN HE IS SURPRISED BY THAT!

TOP 10 TOOLS OF A SUPER VILLAIN

10 Equipment that causes lots of destruction or even explosions

9 A good monologue

VILLAINS LOVE MONOLOGUING!

8 An unlimited amount of money

ALL THAT SUPER TECH IS EXPENSIVE!

7 An incredibly cool vehicle, usually with an escape pod

6 A catchy motto

"WHEN EVERYONE IS SUPER, NO ONE WILL BE."
—SYNDROME

5 Equipment for holding your enemies

THE BEST SUPER VILLAINS WAIT TO MONOLOGUE UNTIL THE HERO IS TRAPPED.

4 A control room with a wall-size screen

3 A convincing disguise

2 A clever name like Bomb Voyage, the Screenslaver, or the Underminer

1

A SECRET LAIR

JACK-JACK'S TOP 10 INCREDIBLE MOMENTS

10 He plays keep-away with the babysitter.

IS IT CHEATING IF YOU CAN FLOAT THROUGH WALLS?

9 Syndrome almost drops him when he turns to heavy metal.

8 Any time he teleports.

HE MUST BE THE BEST PEEKABOO PLAYER.

7 He becomes a sticky goo ball.

BABIES ARE MESSY, BUT JACK-JACK BRINGS IT TO ANOTHER LEVEL.

6

He saves his mom from the Screenslaver.

GOODBYE, HYPNO-GOGGLES!

∧∧∧∧∧
DID YOU KNOW?

Jack-Jack was supposed to turn into a goo ball in *The Incredibles*. But the animation team couldn't make it work in time. They made it happen in *Incredibles 2*.

5

He gets on Edna's good side by copying her look.

4

He traps the raccoon all by himself.

3

Any time he sneezes.

WATCH OUT FOR LASER BEAMS, FIREBALLS, AND LIGHTNING BOLTS!

2

He turns into a monster when he wants a cookie.

1

EVERY TIME HE GIGGLES.

CUTEST LAUGH EVER!

TOP 10 REASONS EDNA IS INCREDIBLE

10 She's a famous fashion designer.

BUT SHE'S NOT IMPRESSED WITH SUPERMODELS.

9 She loves chatting with Supers, especially Elastigirl.

8 She forbids capes.

SHE'S LEARNED FROM HER MISTAKES.

7 She has an impressive security system.

6

She tells people exactly how she feels.

^^^^^
DID YOU KNOW?

In *The Incredibles*, Edna puts her hand through a tear in Mr. Incredible's Supersuit. This scene may look simple, but the animation needed for it was *incredibly* complicated. The scene was actually more difficult to create than the plane explosion scene!

5

Her house is as fashionable as she is.

IT ALSO CONTAINS HER SUPER HIGH-TECH LAB!

4

She may be short, but she can intimidate even the toughest Super.

3

She's a wonderful babysitter.

2

She engineers amazing technology in fabulous Supersuits.

1

SHE IS A CREATIVE PROBLEM SOLVER.

25

TOP 10 SUPER POWERS YOU CAN HAVE

10

COURAGE

Heroes don't let their fears stop them.

9

OPTIMISM

Heroes never give up hope.

8

CURIOSITY

Heroes never stop learning.

7

HONOR

Heroes work for the greater good.

>>

6

TRUSTWORTHINESS

Heroes are dependable.

5

HELPFULNESS

Heroes want to be useful.

4

RESOURCEFULNESS

Heroes solve problems in creative ways.

3

PERSISTENCE

Heroes don't give up if something goes wrong.

2

COOPERATION

Heroes need to work well with others.

1

COMPASSION

Heroes care about others.

QUIZ BREAK!

Are you a superfan of the Incredibles? Take this quiz and find out!

1

WHY DOESN'T EVELYN LIKE SUPERS?

A Supers keep us weak.
B She is jealous of the Supers' powers.
C Supers are show-offs.
D She doesn't like people in masks.

2

WHAT COMPOSER DOES THE BABYSITTER PLAY FOR JACK-JACK?

A Beethoven
B Chopin
C Mozart
D Tchaikovsky

3

WHAT DOES EDNA USE TO PASS HER LAB SECURITY?

A Voice recognition
B Hand scan
C A secret code
D All of the above

WHAT IS THE NAME OF VIOLET'S CRUSH?

4

A Syndrome
B Brad Bird
C Tony Rydinger
D Rick Dicker

5

WHERE WAS THE INCREDIBILE?

A In a junkyard
B In someone's car collection
C At the bottom of a lake
D On an army base

6

WHAT IS FROZONE'S REAL NAME?

A Samuel
B Lucius
C Jonathan
D Sean

7

WHICH VILLAIN USES THE TUNNELER?

A Bomb Voyage
B Syndrome
C The Underminer
D The Procrastinator

8

WHICH SUPER HELPS ELASTIGIRL GET IN EVELYN'S PLANE?

A Krushauer
B Brick
C He-lectrix
D Voyd

9

WHAT IS SYNDROME DEFEATED BY?

A His cape
B His rocket boots
C His remote-control gloves
D His robots

10

WHICH OF THESE IS NOT ONE OF JACK-JACK'S POWERS?

A Shape-shifting
B Super speed
C Teleportation
D Replication

TOP 10 RULES FOR BEING A TOY

10 You live in the world of people.

9 Don't move around people.

8 Don't speak around people.

UNLESS, OF COURSE, THEY'VE PULLED YOUR STRING.

7 Make sure people find you where they left you.

6

You can speak and move on your own around animals.

THEY WON'T TELL YOUR SECRET!

∧∧∧∧∧

DID YOU KNOW?

The *Toy Story* animators loved thinking creatively when they played with their toys as kids. They experimented with their toys, changed them, and tried to think of new and different ways to play with them.

5

Be there for your kid, even though your kid might leave you one day.

4

Don't scare your kid.

YOUR JOB IS TO HELP YOUR KID FEEL SAFE.

3

Play the way your kid wants to play.

2

Make your kid happy.

THAT'S WHAT YOU'RE HERE FOR, AFTER ALL.

1

LOVE YOUR KID.

THAT'S WHAT YOUR KID IS HERE FOR, AFTER ALL.

31

TOP 10 ALIEN ADVENTURES

10

Acting in *Romeo and Juliet* with Mr. Pricklepants.

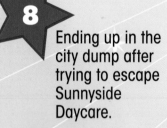

9

Being chosen by "The claaaaaaaw!"

8

Ending up in the city dump after trying to escape Sunnyside Daycare.

7

Getting kidnapped by Evil Dr. Porkchop.

"THAT'S MR. EVIL DR. PORKCHOP TO YOU!"

6 Playing with toddlers in the Caterpillar Room at Sunnyside Daycare.

5 Flying out the window of the Pizza Planet truck on the race to the airport.

HOLD ON! MR. POTATO HEAD WILL SAVE YOU!

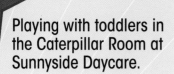

4 ← Becoming a chew toy for Sid's dog Scud.

3 Driving the getaway car for One-Eyed Bart and One-Eyed Betty.

STEP ON IT!

2 Going through the "mystic portal" at the airport.

1 ←

USING A CRANE TO SAVE THE OTHER TOYS FROM THE FURNACE.

THEY WERE ETERNALLY GRATEFUL.

TOP 10 THINGS YOU NEED TO BE A COWBOY SHERIFF

10 A pair of blue jeans and a plaid western shirt

9 A desire to do the right thing

8 A red bandana

IT KEEPS DUST FROM THE TRAIL OFF YOUR NECK.

7 A belt with a big buckle

THE BIGGER THE BUCKLE, THE BETTER!

6

Some good sheriff catchphrases, like "Reach for the sky!"

5

A trusty horse to ride

GIDDYAP, BULLSEYE!

4

The right cowboy hat

3

A cowgirl for a friend

IT'S EVEN BETTER IF SHE YODELS.

2

A pair of cowboy boots with spurs

1

A STAR-SHAPED SHERIFF'S BADGE

⟸

TOP 10 THINGS YOU NEED TO BE A SPACE RANGER

10 The determination to help and protect people

9 A jet pack

8 A spaceship

7 Arms with karate-chop action for showing off your martial arts training

OR CHOPPING BRANCHES OUT OF THE WAY.

6

A flip-open voice recorder for mission entries

5

A job working for Star Command

4

A space ranger badge

IT LETS EVERYONE IN THE GALAXY KNOW YOU'RE ONE OF THE GOOD GUYS.

3

Pop-out glider wings with landing lights

USEFUL FOR BOTH FLYING AND FALLING.

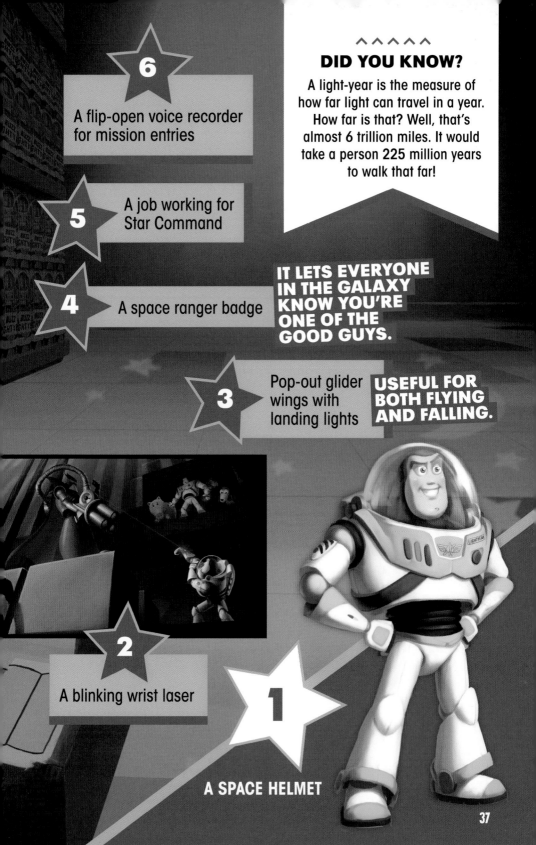

2

A blinking wrist laser

1

A SPACE HELMET

TOY STORY'S TOP 10 ACTION SCENES

10 Stinky Pete traps Woody and won't let him leave.

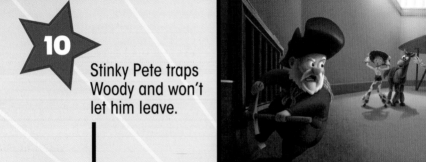

9 The toys work together to scare Sid.

8 Buzz and Woody get trapped in Sid's room.

7 Lotso drags Woody into a dumpster, and the other toys jump in to save him.

THAT'S WHAT FRIENDS DO!

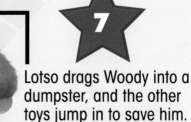

6 Buzz battles the Evil Emperor Zurg on top of the elevator.

WHAT'S UP? SOMEBODY IS GOING DOWN!

5 Woody and Buzz try to catch up to the moving van.

THEY "DROP IN" ON ANDY JUST IN TIME!

4 It's the good guys versus the bad guys in a Wild West showdown to save a train full of orphans.

2 In an epic battle, Zurg blasts Buzz in half.

OUCH!

∧∧∧∧∧
DID YOU KNOW?

Pixar animators had a scare when their computer system suddenly began deleting all the work they'd done on *Toy Story 2*. Fortunately, one of the animators had copied the files and taken them home. She saved the day—and the movie!

3 Buzz and the other toys rescue Woody, Jessie, and Bullseye at the airport.

1

WOODY, BUZZ, AND THEIR FRIENDS GET CLOSER AND CLOSER TO THE FLAMES OF THE FURNACE.

LUCKILY, THE ALIENS SAVED THEM WITH A HELPING HAND, ER, CLAW.

TOP 10 TOY STORY QUOTES

10 "Ride like the wind, Bullseye!"

YEE-HAW, WOODY!

9 "This is no time to panic." —Buzz
"This is the *perfect* time to panic!" —Woody

8 "You are a sad, strange little man, and you have my pity." —Buzz

7 "The important thing is that we stick together." —Buzz

6

When Buzz starts speaking Spanish to Jessie:
"Did you fix Buzz?" —Jessie
"Eh, sort of." —Hamm

^ ^ ^ ^ ^
DID YOU KNOW?

Infinity is something that has no beginning, no end, and no limits. Some astronomers think the universe has no beginning or end. They think space may stretch out forever in all directions. Hard to get beyond that, isn't it?

5

"This isn't flying. This is falling with style!"

EITHER WAY, IT'S A GOOD THING BUZZ HAS THOSE WINGS!

↳»

4

"But the thing that makes Woody special is he'll never give up on you . . . ever."

ANDY KNOWS HE HAS A FRIEND IN WOODY.

3

"You. Are. A. TOY!" —Woody

2

"Over in that house is a kid who thinks you are the greatest. And it's not because you're a Space Ranger. It's because you're a toy. You are his toy." —Woody

1

"TO INFINITY AND BEYOND!"

WE ALL KNOW THIS ONE FROM BUZZ!

TOP 10 TIMES TOY STORY MADE US CRY

10

When Chuckles tells the story of how he, Big Baby, and Lotso ended up at Sunnyside Daycare.

9

Buster changes and grows older just as Andy does. When Andy leaves for college, he hopes Buster will still be around the next time he comes home.

8

Woody chooses to stay at Al's and refuses to go back to Andy with the other toys.

OH, WOODY, PLEASE GO WITH YOUR OLD FRIENDS.

7

Then Woody realizes he'll miss Andy if he doesn't go home.

OH, WOODY, DON'T LEAVE YOUR NEW FRIENDS AT AL'S!

6 Buzz realizes that he's a toy.

HE HAS A BROKEN ARM . . . AND A BROKEN HEART.

5 Woody decides to leave Sunnyside and says goodbye to everyone, including Bullseye.

4 Jessie tells Woody about Emily outgrowing her.

DOES ANYONE HAVE A TISSUE?

3 When all the toys quietly hold hands (and paws and hooves and claws) as they get closer to the flames of the furnace.

2 When Andy gives his toys to Bonnie.

1

^ ^ ^ ^ ^
DID YOU KNOW?

Music can help people connect to their emotions. Music often tells a movie audience whether a scene is sad, exciting, funny, or scary. The songs from the Toy Story movies also help the audience know what the characters think and feel.

THE TOYS WATCH ANDY DRIVE AWAY AS HE HEADS OFF TO COLLEGE. "SO LONG, PARTNER . . ."

⬅

43

TOY STORY'S TOP 10 FUNNY MOMENTS

10 Woody knocks Buzz's space helmet off, and Buzz thinks he can't breathe.

9 Jessie skateboards down a ramp, yodels, launches herself onto the doorknob, and opens the door so Buster can go outside "for a little private time."

BUZZ IS SO IMPRESSED THAT HIS WINGS POP UP!

8 When Woody and Buzz meet each other for the first time.

"HELLOOO—AHH!"

7 The aliens' excitement about being chosen by the claw.

OOOOOH!

6

Tour Guide Barbie drives the toys through Al's Toy Barn.

BUCKLE UP!

5

Woody asks Buzz to give him a hand in Sid's room, and Buzz throws him a whole arm.

GOOD ONE, BUZZ.

4

The toys work together to drive the Planet Pizza truck to the airport.

3

The toys use orange traffic cones to "safely" cross the street.

2

Spanish-mode Buzz dancing with Jessie. *¡Olé!*

1

BUZZ, WEARING A PINK APRON AND A FLOWERED HAT, DROWNS HIS SORROWS AT A TEA PARTY.

"YOU SEE THE HAT? I AM MRS. NESBITT!" 45

TOP 10 THINGS ANDY LEARNS FROM HIS TOYS

10 HOW TO DECORATE A ROOM

First, a cowboy bedspread and then a space ranger bedspread.

9 HOW TO DEVELOP HIS ARTISTIC SKILLS

Buzz and Woody inspire a lot of Andy's drawings.

8 HOW TO USE HIS IMAGINATION

That's where Evil Dr. Porkchop and One-Eyed Betty come from!

7 HOW TO HAVE HOPE

Woody and Buzz were lost, but they found their way back to him!

6

HOW TO TRUST

Toys are friendly, not scary.

^^^^^
DID YOU KNOW?

Andy isn't the only kid who grows up in the Toy Story movies. Sid grows up to be the garbage collector in *Toy Story 3*. Did you catch that?

5

HOW TO BE CARING

Andy takes good care of his toys. He fixed Woody's torn arm.

4

HOW TO SHARE

Bonnie will have so much fun with Andy's toys!

3

HOW TO BE LOYAL

As Andy says, Woody will never give up on you.

2

HOW TO BE DEPENDABLE

The toys are always there for Andy when he needs them.

1

HOW TO BE GRATEFUL

"THANKS, GUYS."

TOP 10 TOY STORY CONNECTIONS TO OTHER MOVIES

10

THE WIZARD OF OZ

Just like Dorothy, Woody says, "There's no place like home," when he's trying to get out of Sid's room.

9

STAR WARS

The loud breathing sound Buzz makes when wearing his space helmet is similar to Darth Vader's famous breathing sound.

8

A BUG'S LIFE

Heimlich the caterpillar is on one of the branches being chopped by Buzz.

7

STAR WARS: EPISODE V— THE EMPIRE STRIKES BACK

Zurg tells Buzz, "I am your father," which is the same thing Darth Vader says to Luke Skywalker.

6

CARS

A toy car that looks like Lightning McQueen is at Sunnyside Daycare.

5

FINDING NEMO

Bonnie has a bandage with Dory on it, and Dory is in some of the paintings at the day care.

4

THE INCREDIBLES

In *Toy Story 3*, the model jet in Andy's room looks just like the one that Elastigirl pilots to save Mr. Incredible from Syndrome's island.

THE LION KING

2

"Hakuna Matata" is playing on the car radio as Andy, his sister, and his mom drive to their new house.

∧∧∧∧∧

DID YOU KNOW?

The Pizza Planet truck from *Toy Story* shows up in all the Toy Story movies. It appears in lots of other movies too, including *Cars*, *Finding Nemo*, *Inside Out*, and *Coco*. Hidden connections in a movie are called Easter Eggs because you have to hunt for them!

3

A BUG'S LIFE

Mrs. Potato Head is shown reading *A Bug's Life* storybook.

1

CARS

ON THE WAY TO PIZZA PLANET, ANDY'S MOM PULLS INTO A DINOCO GAS STATION.

49

TOP 10 FRIENDSHIP FACTS FROM BUZZ AND WOODY

10 Friends don't always like each other when they first meet.

"LISTEN, LIGHTSNACK, YOU STAY AWAY FROM ANDY. HE'S MINE, AND NO ONE IS TAKING HIM AWAY FROM ME." —WOODY

9 You can have more than one good friend.

ANDY'S NAME IS ON WOODY'S BOOT *AND* BUZZ'S BOOT.

8 Friends give each other a helping hand.

AND SOMETIMES THAT HAND IS ATTACHED TO AN ARM.

7 Friends don't give up on each other.

"THE IMPORTANT THING IS THAT WE STICK TOGETHER." —BUZZ

6

Friends tell each other the truth.

 5

Friends protect each other.

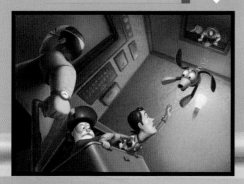

 4

Friends can argue and still be friends.

3

Friends can be different from each other.

FOR EXAMPLE, ONE CAN BE A COWBOY AND ONE CAN BE A SPACE RANGER.

 2

Friends have fun together.

1

THE BEST WAY TO HAVE A GOOD FRIEND IS TO BE A GOOD FRIEND.

YOU'VE GOT A FRIEND IN ME!

QUIZ BREAK!

Find out how much you know about the adventures of Woody, Buzz, and their friends. To the first question and beyond!

1

WOODY SAYS ALL OF THESE PHRASES WHEN YOU PULL HIS STRING, EXCEPT

A "There's a snake in my boot!"
B "Reach for the sky!"
C "You're my favorite deputy!"
D "Howdy, little lady!"

2

WHEN BUZZ FALLS OUT OF THE WINDOW, ANDY'S TOYS TRY TO SAVE HIM WITH

A A yo-yo
B A barrel of monkeys
C A jump rope
D Soldiers

3

BUZZ HAS ALL OF THE FOLLOWING FEATURES EXCEPT

A Chopping action
B A glow-in-the-dark suit
C Flying abilities
D Laser beam light

4

WHEN BUZZ MEETS THE ALIENS AT PIZZA PLANET, WHO OR WHAT DO THEY CLAIM IS THEIR MASTER?

A Buzz
B Zurg
C The claw
D Pizza

5

AL'S TOY BARN COMMERCIALS FEATURE

A Al dressed as a chicken
B Giant stuffed animals
C Al doing the chicken dance
D Al sitting on a rocking horse

6

WHAT IS THE NAME OF JESSIE'S PREVIOUS KID?

A Molly
B Amanda
C Amy
D Emily

7

WHO DID WOODY SAVE FROM THE YARD SALE?

A Wheezy
B Bo's sheep
C Hamm
D Squeaky shark

8

BONNIE FIRST FINDS WOODY

A When she trips over him
B Hanging from a tree
C In a box
D In the Caterpillar Room

9

WHOSE IDEA WAS IT TO CLIMB INSIDE THE SUNNYSIDE DONATION BOX?

A Buzz
B Jessie
C Mr. Potato Head
D Woody

10

WHO RESCUED ANDY'S TOYS AT THE TRI-COUNTY LANDFILL?

A The aliens
B Lotso
C Zurg
D A landfill worker

FROZEN'S TOP 10 FROZEN THINGS

10 The village water fountain

9 The forest on North Mountain

IT'S THE PERFECT PLACE TO BUILD AN ICE PALACE!

8 The waters of the fjord

7 Marshmallow

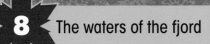

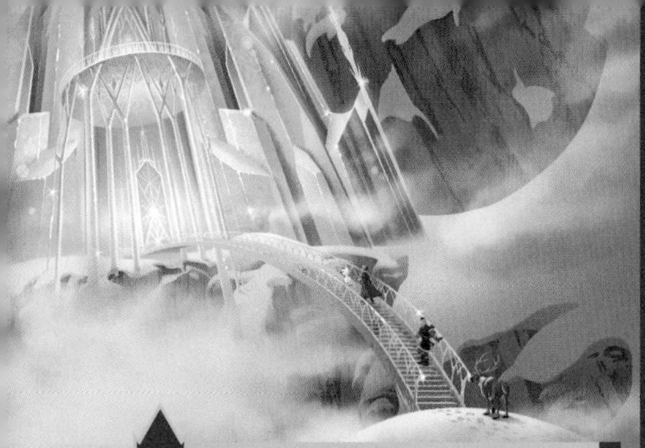

DID YOU KNOW?

The animators for *Frozen* made more than two thousand different snowflake shapes to use in the movie.

6 The stairway leading to Elsa's ice palace

5 Snowgies!

OUR FAVORITE PART OF *FROZEN FEVER*!

4 Anna

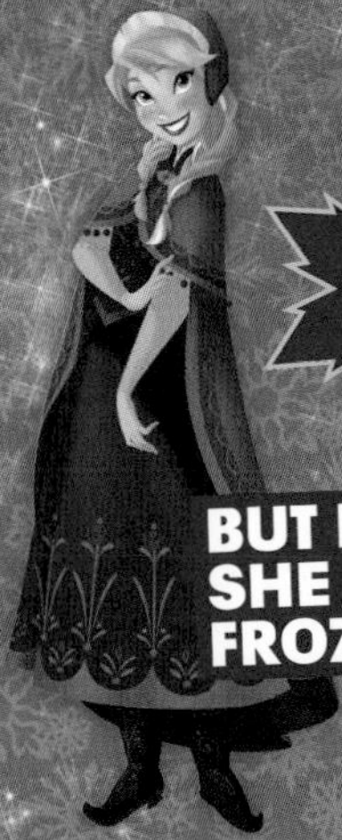

BUT DON'T WORRY. SHE DOESN'T STAY FROZEN FOR LONG!

3 All of Arendelle until Elsa learns to control her powers

2 Elsa's ice palace

1 OLAF

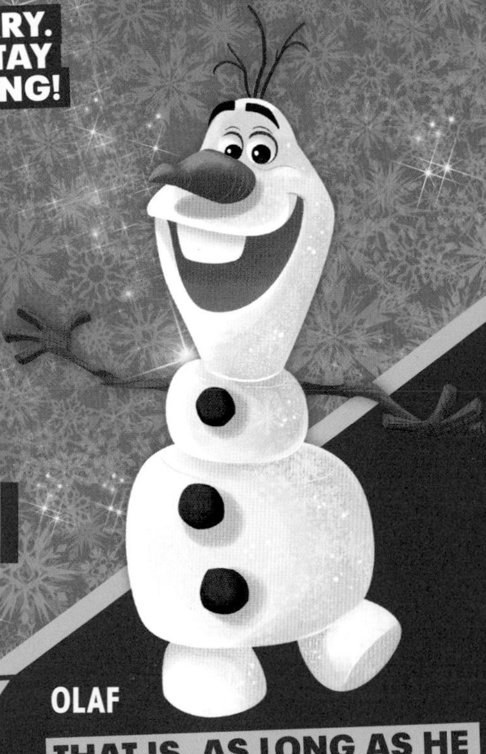

THAT IS, AS LONG AS HE STAYS AWAY FROM FIRE.

TOP 10 REASONS ANNA IS A GOOD SISTER

10 She likes a lot of the same things as her sister. **LIKE CHOCOLATE AND PLAYING IN THE SNOW.**

9 She's musical. **SHE'LL EVEN SING THROUGH A KEYHOLE IF SHE HAS TO SO SHE CAN TALK WITH HER SISTER!**

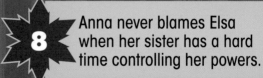

8 Anna never blames Elsa when her sister has a hard time controlling her powers.

7 She's caring.

6

Anna doesn't let other people's fear change how she feels about Elsa.

∧ ∧ ∧ ∧ ∧
DID YOU KNOW?
The filmmakers who worked on *Frozen* interviewed women about what it was like to grow up with a sister. They wanted to make Anna and Elsa's relationship as accurate as possible.

5

Anna believes in Elsa, even when Elsa doesn't believe in herself.

4

Anna is determined to help her sister no matter what other people say.

3 She's brave.

ANNA IS WILLING TO FACE DANGER TO RESCUE HER SISTER.

2 Anna loves to play, especially with Elsa.

DO YOU WANNA BUILD A SNOWMAN?

1

ANNA LOVES HER BIG SISTER.

57

TOP 10 TIMES ELSA WAS STRONG

10 When she takes off her gloves at the coronation ceremony.

EVEN THOUGH SHE WAS AFRAID HER POWERS MIGHT BE REVEALED.

9 When she gives Anna advice about Hans that Anna might not want to hear.

8 When she accepts her responsibility to become queen after her parents pass away.

WHAT A BIG RESPONSIBILITY.

7 When she decides to live on a lonely mountain on her own to keep the people of Arendelle safe from her powers.

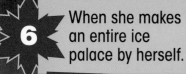

6 When she makes an entire ice palace by herself.

HER POWERS ARE SO AMAZING!

5 When she fights off Hans and the Duke's men when they come to the ice palace.

4 When she uses her icy powers to let the citizens of Arendelle play in the snow and ice.

MAKING AN ENTIRE ICE RINK IS NO SMALL THING!

3 When she breaks through the wall of her prison cell.

2 When she learns to live without her parents even though it's hard.

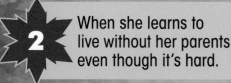

1 WHEN SHE FINDS THE COURAGE TO STOP HIDING WHO SHE REALLY IS.

FROZEN'S TOP 10 MUSICAL MOMENTS

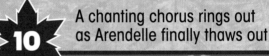

10 A chanting chorus rings out as Arendelle finally thaws out

9 The ice harvesters deliver a cold warning about a frozen heart

BRRRRR!

8 Kristoff and Sven's "duet" about reindeer versus people

7 The trolls "fix up" Kristoff

THEY ARE SOOO HELPFUL!

6

Anna begs Elsa to come back to the kingdom, and Elsa begs Anna to just leave her alone

5

Olaf imagines what summer would be like

JUST THINKING ABOUT IT MAKES HIM SO HAPPY!

4

Anna and Hans open the door to love and maybe even marriage

WAIT, WHAT?

3

Anna is so excited on coronation day that she can hardly stand it

2

Anna sings into the keyhole to ask Elsa to come out and play

1

ELSA DECIDES TO LET GO OF HER FEAR AND BE HERSELF

TOP 10 OLAF QUOTES

10 "Oh, look at that. I've been impaled."

9 "Hands down, this is the best day of my life . . . and quite possibly the last." **HE SAYS AS HE'S MELTING.**

8 "Love is putting someone else's needs before yours."

7 "Why isn't she knocking? Do you think she knows how to knock?" **IT'S WHAT'S BEHIND THE DOOR THAT'S MAKING HER NERVOUS, OLAF.**

6 "I like warm hugs."

5 "I always wanted a nose! It's so cute. It's like a little baby unicorn!"

OR A SNACK FOR SVEN—BE CAREFUL, OLAF!

4 "Whoa, so this is heat. I love it. Oh, but don't touch it!"

3 "And who's the funky-looking donkey over there? . . . And who's the reindeer?"

ANNA AND OLAF MAY HAVE HAD A SLIGHT MISUNDERSTANDING THERE.

2 "Oh, I don't know why, but I've always loved the idea of summer and sun and all things hot."

1

"SOME PEOPLE ARE WORTH MELTING FOR— JUST MAYBE NOT RIGHT THIS SECOND."

FROZEN'S TOP 10 DRAMATIC MOMENTS

10 Elsa's quick change into her new icy dress.

9 The Duke's men shoot at Elsa in the ice palace as she fights them off.

8 Grand Pabbie warns young Elsa about her powers.

7 Kristoff and Sven race back to Arendelle to save Anna.

HURRY, KRISTOFF!

6 Young Elsa accidentally hits young Anna in the head with ice.

THE FIRST SIGN OF TROUBLE . . .

∧∧∧∧∧

DID YOU KNOW?

Kristoff makes a snow anchor to hold a rope so that he and Anna can get away from Marshmallow. A snow anchor is a real thing. It's a patch of snow that's then circled with a rope.

5 Hans reveals his plans to kill Elsa. Then he locks Anna in the cold library.

NOT A GOOD GUY AFTER ALL!

4

Elsa accidentally freezes all of Arendelle.

3 Wolves chase Kristoff, Anna, and Sven through the forest.

2 Marshmallow chases Kristoff, Anna, and Olaf off a cliff.

1

ANNA SAVES ELSA'S LIFE BY BLOCKING HANS'S SWORD JUST AS SHE FREEZES.

DOESN'T GET MUCH MORE DRAMATIC THAN THAT!

FROZEN'S TOP 10 OUTFITS

10 Anna and Kristoff dressed in troll fashion, wearing capes and headdresses made from plants

9 The Duke of Weselton's coronation outfit

INCLUDING THE FRINGE AND WHITE GLOVES THAT HELP HIM SHOW OFF HIS DANCING SKILLS.

8 Sven's antler accessories from the frozen forest

7 Oaken's Nordic knitwear

6

Hans's coronation outfit

IT MAKES HIM LOOK LIKE ONE OF THE GOOD GUYS, DOESN'T IT?

∧∧∧∧∧
DID YOU KNOW?

Animators studied the way real fabrics felt and moved as they designed the outfits for *Frozen*. Then they could make computer drawings of clothing for *Frozen* that look and move just as real clothing does.

5

Kristoff's no-nonsense mountain man clothes

4

Anna's warm winter travel clothes

SHE KNOWS HOW TO BUNDLE UP IN STYLE!

3

Anna's coronation gown in shades of yellow and green

THE WARM, FRESH COLORS OF SUMMER.

1

2

Elsa's coronation gown, in darker, cooler shades of winter

ELSA'S ICY GOWN, CAPE, AND SHOES

IT'S THE ULTIMATE COOL OUTFIT!

TOP 10 THINGS TO DO IN ARENDELLE

10 Learn to harvest ice.

9 Enjoy a ride on Kristoff's fancy new sled.

BRING A CARROT FOR SVEN, AND ENJOY THAT CUP HOLDER!

8 Hike to the realm of the trolls.

WATCH OUT FOR THE ROCKS!

7 Visit Wandering Oaken's Trading Post and Sauna.

6

Meet lots of interesting people down by the water when ships come in to port.

5 See the northern lights.

4 Go to a ball hosted by Anna and Elsa.

3 Take a tour of Elsa's ice palace.

CAREFUL ON THE STAIRS—THEY'RE A LITTLE SLIPPERY.

2 Say hello to a friendly snowman who travels with his own personal flurry.

1

GO ICE-SKATING ALL YEAR.

DON'T FORGET TO PACK YOUR SKATES!

OUR TOP 10 FAVORITE THINGS ABOUT *FROZEN'S* TROLLS

10 They are good singers.

9 They wear cloaks made of moss.

8 They can grow mushrooms on their bodies.

HOW DO THEY DO THAT?

7 They are small, but they can roll and stack themselves if they need to be taller.

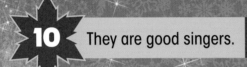
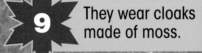

6 Their crystal necklaces glow.

THEY LOOK JUST LIKE THE NORTHERN LIGHTS!

∧ ∧ ∧ ∧ ∧
DID YOU KNOW?
The swirling designs on the trolls' clothes are meant to look like lichen. Lichen is a small, slow-growing plant that lives on rocks and trees.

5 Family is very important to them.

4 They can make themselves look like rocks.

ROCK ON, TROLLS!

3 They can organize a wedding in a hurry.

2 They are love experts.

DO YOU NEED A HEALING HUG?

1

THEY ARE KIND AND WILL HELP ANYONE IN NEED.

TOP 10 REASONS WHY KRISTOFF IS AWESOME

10

He knows how to harvest ice.

ICE IS HIS LIFE!

9

He's always prepared for winter.

8

He's an excellent sled driver.

7

He eats healthy food.

A LOT OF CARROTS . . .

6

He is not afraid to explore new places.

5

He truly appreciates a palace made of ice.

"NOW *THAT'S* ICE. I MIGHT CRY."

∧∧∧∧∧

DID YOU KNOW?

The story for *Frozen* is inspired by a fairy tale called *The Snow Queen*, written by Hans Christian Andersen in 1844. If you say the names of four of *Frozen*'s main characters together fast—Hans, Kristoff, Anna, Sven—it sounds like Hans Christian Andersen.

4

He'll help you escape from a snow monster.

3

He was raised by trolls, who taught him to help others.

2

He has a reindeer for a best friend.

GOOD OLD SVEN.

1

HE RACES ACROSS A FROZEN FJORD TO TRY TO SAVE THE PERSON HE LOVES.

TOP 10 TIMES *FROZEN* MELTS YOUR HEART

10 The doors of the castle open, and Anna finally gets to go outside.

HELLO, SUNSHINE!

9 Every time Sven acts like a puppy instead of a reindeer.

WHO KNEW A REINDEER COULD BE SO LOVABLE?

8 Olaf imagines all the joys of summer.

7 Kristoff goes home to see the trolls.

AND HE'S BROUGHT A GIRL!

6

Anna and Elsa realize that true love can take many forms.

∧ ∧ ∧ ∧ ∧
DID YOU KNOW?

Walt Disney wanted to make a movie like this for a long time. He first thought about it in 1943, but *Frozen* didn't come out until 2013. Sometimes it takes a long time to get a story just right!

5

Elsa realizes she can be herself without being afraid.

4

Kristoff and Sven rush through the storm and across the frozen fjord to save Anna.

3

Anna uses the last of her energy to save Elsa.

NOW THAT'S TRUE LOVE.

2

Elsa comes to understand that love is stronger than fear.

AN ACT OF TRUE LOVE IS STRONG ENOUGH TO THAW A FROZEN HEART.

1

OLAF WARMS ANNA BY THE FIRE (AND HIMSELF JUST A LITTLE TOO MUCH) AS HE EXPLAINS TRUE LOVE.

QUIZ BREAK!

How many fabulous *Frozen* facts do you know?
Take this quiz to find out!

1

EVERYONE KNOWS WHO OLAF IS. WHAT IS THE NAME OF THE OTHER SNOWMAN ELSA CREATES TO PROTECT HER ICE PALACE?

A Snowball
B Marshmallow
C Rocky
D Frostor

2

WHAT IS ANNA AND ELSA'S FAVORITE FOOD?

A Cupcakes
B Chocolate
C Carrot cake
D Cherry pie

3

WHICH FROZEN CHARACTER SAYS, "ICE IS MY LIFE"?

A Oaken
B Marshmallow
C Elsa
D Kristoff

4

WHO SAYS, "THAT'S NO BLIZZARD. THAT'S MY SISTER"?

A Anna
B Elsa
C Hans
D Kristoff

5

WHICH REAL-LIFE PLACE ON EARTH IS THE INSPIRATION FOR ARENDELLE?

A Norway
B Sweden
C Denmark
D The Netherlands

6

WHEN ANNA AND ELSA OPEN UP THE CASTLE FOR ELSA'S CORONATION, WHICH FAMOUS DISNEY PRINCESS IS AMONG THE GUESTS?

A Aurora
B Rapunzel
C Merida
D Belle

7

WHERE DOES ELSA CREATE HER ICE PALACE?

A North Mountain
B The South Pole
C Dark Valley
D The Far Peak

8

HOW DO ANNA, KRISTOFF, AND OLAF GET TO THE DOORS OF THE ICE PALACE?

A An ice slide
B A secret passage
C A long staircase
D By climbing a wall

9

WHO CONVINCES KRISTOFF TO GO BACK TO ARENDELLE TO HELP ANNA?

A Elsa
B Olaf
C Sven
D The Trolls

10

WHAT ACT OF TRUE LOVE SAVES ANNA FROM AN ICY FATE?

A Kristoff coming back to save her
B Olaf starting a fire
C A kiss from Hans
D Anna jumping in front of a sword to save her sister

TOP 10 SCARIEST MOMENTS IN *SNOW WHITE*

10 Entering the Dwarfs' messy cottage.

ALL THE DUST AND COBWEBS!

9 When the Evil Queen talks to the Magic Mirror.

8 The Huntsman comes at Snow White with a knife.

7 The animals try to save Snow White from the Evil Queen, but she shoos them away.

6 The Evil Queen tries to stop the Dwarfs with a boulder.

5 When the Evil Queen dips an apple into the potion, and it looks like a skull.

CREEPY!

4 The Evil Queen kicks the skeleton in her dungeon.

 3 When Snow White is lost in the dark forest.

 2 Snow White accepts the poisoned apple.

DON'T TAKE A BITE!

1

THE EVIL QUEEN CHANGES INTO THE OLD HAG.

OH, THAT CACKLE!

TOP 10 MOST CHALLENGING PARTS OF CINDERELLA'S LIFE

10 Getting only a few minutes of free time

9 Walking up all those stairs to her bedroom

AT LEAST IT'S GOOD EXERCISE.

8 Helping her stepsisters get ready for a ball that she's not allowed to attend

7

Doing laundry every day

6 Protecting her little friends from Lucifer

5 Shoes that fall off too easily

SHE LOSES HER SHOE THREE DIFFERENT TIMES!

4 Learning to balance breakfast trays on her head

THAT MUST HAVE TAKEN A LOT OF PRACTICE!

3 The chiming clock wakes her up from beautiful dreams

2 Magic that only lasts until midnight

1

BEING TREATED LIKE A SERVANT BY HER STEPMOTHER AND STEPSISTERS

TOP 10 REASONS AURORA WOULD BE A FUN FRIEND

10 It would be awesome to visit her quirky aunts.

9 The stories about her dreams are so wonderful.

8 She probably knows where to find the tastiest berries in the forest.

7 Best karaoke partner ever!

HER VOICE IS AMAZING.

6 She loves going on fun nature walks.

5 She is kind to everyone.

4 She has a secret identity.

KIND OF LIKE A SUPERHERO!

3 Her other friends are adorable forest critters.

2 She loves to dance.

↳ ≫

1

SHE HAS A PLAYFUL IMAGINATION.

THE LITTLE MERMAID'S TOP 10 FUNNIEST MOMENTS

10

Scuttle tries to figure out what is different about Ariel after she's become human.

SHE'S GOT LEGS, DUDE!

9

Chef Louis and Sebastian's chase scene.

8

Ariel talks to Prince Eric's statue.

7

Scuttle tries to hear Prince Eric's heartbeat by listening to his foot.

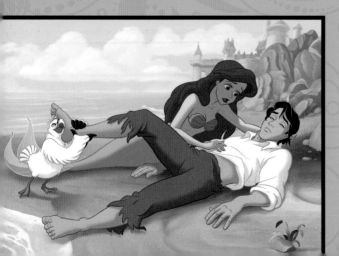

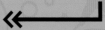

6 Prince Eric can barely hold on when Ariel drives the carriage.

HIS FACE IS PRICELESS!

5 Sebastian tries to teach Ariel how to bat her eyelashes and pucker her lips.

4 Ariel's face when Prince Eric tries to guess her name.

3 Scuttle tries to sing a romantic song.

GOOD THING SEBASTIAN TOOK OVER.

2 Ariel combs her hair with a fork at the dinner table.

1 SEBASTIAN AND HIS SEA FRIENDS FINISH THE "UNDER THE SEA" SPECTACULAR ONLY TO FIND THAT ARIEL HAS SWUM AWAY.

TOP 10 TIMES *BEAUTY AND THE BEAST* TOOK OUR BREATH AWAY

10 Belle running to the top of the hill and looking out at the incredible view.

9 The Beast saving Belle from the wolves.

8 Seeing the library for the first time!
SO MANY BOOKS.

7

Belle discovering the magic rose.

SO THAT'S WHY THE WEST WING IS FORBIDDEN.

6 The Beast deciding to let Gaston go.

DID YOU KNOW?

Every line in the song "Beauty and the Beast" has only five syllables. The songwriters wanted it to be simple.

5 Belle and the Beast dancing in the ballroom.

4 Belle offering to trade places with her father.

WOW, SHE'S BRAVE.

3 The Beast becoming human again.

SEEING EVERYBODY ELSE AS HUMANS IS PRETTY COOL TOO!

2

Belle and the Beast seeing each other on the ballroom stairs.

1

THE MOST SPECTACULAR DINNER SHOW EVER!

TOP 10 LINES FROM *ALADDIN*

10

"Jafar, Jafar, he's our man. If he can't do it, GREAT!" —Genie

9

"I must find this one, this diamond in the rough." —Jafar

8

"Phenomenal cosmic power . . . itty-bitty living space." —Genie

7

"Unhand him, by order of the princess."

JASMINE BEING A BOSS.

6

"The law is wrong."

JASMINE BEING UNAFRAID TO SAY WHAT SHE BELIEVES.

5 "Do you trust me?"

HMMM, PRINCE ALI SOUNDS A LOT LIKE ALADDIN.

4 "From this day forth, the Princess shall marry whomever she deems worthy."

SULTAN GIVING JASMINE THE POWER SHE DESERVES.

3

"Ten thousand years will give you such a crick in the neck." —Genie

2 "Genie, I wish for your freedom."

ALADDIN IS TRUE TO HIS WORD.

1

"I AM NOT A PRIZE TO BE WON!" —JASMINE

THE TOP 10 THINGS POCAHONTAS MADE US APPRECIATE ABOUT NATURE

10 Nature isn't just a resource for us to use.

WE ALSO HAVE A RESPONSIBILITY TO PROTECT IT.

9 Trees in the forest can provide shelter and shade.

8 Nature is a beautiful and colorful place.

7 The river is perfect for transportation.

6 Tall trees are great places to check out what's happening.

5 There is always so much more to explore in the wild.

WHICH RIVER PATH WOULD YOU TAKE?

4 Lakes and rivers are great swimming pools!

3 Animals can be loyal friends!

2 Going where the wind takes you can lead to amazing places.

1

NATURE HAS A LOT OF ANSWERS IF YOU JUST LISTEN.

GRANDMOTHER WILLOW IS SO WISE!

MULAN'S TOP 10 "YOU GO, GIRL!" MOMENTS

10 Mulan keeps training until she can run faster than everyone else can.

9 She beats Captain Li Shang in their training fight.

8 When she cuts off her hair with a sword.

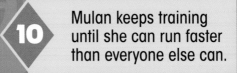

7 She goes back to warn Shang and the Emperor about the Huns.

6 She waits to shoot the canon until just the right moment.

5

When she fends off Shan-Yu with only a fan.

SHE'S GOT SKILLS!

∧∧∧∧∧
DID YOU KNOW?

The computer program that artists used to animate large groups of soldiers in *Mulan* is called Attila. It was named after an ancient Hun ruler.

4

She decides to protect her father and defend her family's honor.

3

She is the first one to figure out how to reach the top of the pole.

USES HER MIND AND HER MUSCLES!

⌐——⟫

2

The Emperor bows to Mulan (and so does everyone else).

1

SHE SAVES HERSELF AND SHANG FROM FALLING OFF A CLIFF WHILE ON HORSEBACK.

CAN'T TOP THAT!

93

TIANA'S TOP 10 ACTS OF PERSISTENCE

 10 She keeps tweaking recipes until they are just perfect.

 9 She works two waitressing jobs to achieve her dream of owning a restaurant.

8 She encourages Naveen not to give up by teaching him to mince mushrooms.

SHE KNOWS HE CAN DO THINGS FOR HIMSELF.

 7 She's not discouraged that the mill is so run down.

SHE'S GOT VISION! BRINGS IT TO ANOTHER LEVEL.

6

She doesn't fall for
Dr. Facillier's offer.

5 She learns
how to dance.

She keeps on
cooking even
when she's a frog.

4

3 She helps Naveen
appreciate hard work.

**AND HE TEACHES HER
TO ENJOY LIFE.**

2 She gets turned into a frog
but still works to make her
dreams come true!

1

**SHE LEARNS TO NEVER
LOSE SIGHT OF WHAT'S
REALLY IMPORTANT.**

RAPUNZEL'S
TOP 10 FIRSTS

10 She saves a life.
LUCKY FLYNN!

9 She makes human friends.

8 She trains a horse.
MAXIMUS WOULD DO ANYTHING FOR HER.

7

She gets a major haircut.

AND BECOMES BRUNETTE TOO.

6 She swims underwater.
SHE'S A QUICK LEARNER!

5 She discovers a new way to use a frying pan.

DID YOU KNOW?

Rapunzel's chameleon was based on an animator's pet chameleon named Pascal. Chameleons change their coloring to communicate with other animals.

4 She touches grass.
NOW THAT'S PURE JOY!

3 She meets her real parents.
SHE'S FOUND PEOPLE THAT TRULY CARE FOR HER.

2 She stands up to Mother Gothel.

1

SHE SEES THE LANTERNS UP CLOSE.

TOP 10 THINGS TO DO WITH MERIDA IN DUNBROCH

10 Learn some Scottish.
CRIVENS!

9

Listen to King Fergus's stories.

8 Learn to rock climb.
MERIDA CAN CLIMB SO HIGH!

7 Talk to Queen Elinor about what it was like to be a bear.

6

Explore the ancient ruins of Mor'du's lair.

^^^^^

DID YOU KNOW?

The animators traveled to Scotland to study the country's landscapes and castles. The Standing Stones in *Brave* were inspired by the real-life Calanais Stones on the Isle of Lewis.

5 Try to keep up with Merida's playful little brothers.

4 Learn to embroider a tapestry.
WHAT A BIG PROJECT.

3 Ride horses across the open country.

2 Learn archery.
MERIDA'S GOT AMAZING SKILLS!

──────►►

1

SLEEP IN A CASTLE.

QUIZ BREAK!

How well do you know Disney princesses? Take this quiz and find out!

1

WHICH PRINCESSES HAVE SIBLINGS?

A. Tiana and Merida
B. Ariel and Jasmine
C. Merida and Ariel
D. Cinderella and Tiana

2

WHAT IS THE NAME OF JASMINE'S TIGER?

A. Stripes
B. Abul
C. Rajah
D. Iago

3

WHAT KIND OF PIE IS SNOW WHITE BAKING FOR THE DWARFS WHEN THE OLD HAG APPEARS?

A. gooseberry
B. apple
C. blueberry
D. pumpkin

WHICH DISNEY PRINCESS IS THE ONLY ONE WHO DOESN'T SING IN HER MOVIE?

4

A. Jasmine
B. Mulan
C. Aurora
D. Merida

5 WHO IS THE FIRST ENCHANTED OBJECT TO SPEAK DIRECTLY TO BELLE IN BEAST'S CASTLE?

A. Chip
B. Cogsworth
C. Lumiere
D. Mrs. Potts

6 WHAT NAME DO THE FAIRIES GIVE TO PRINCESS AURORA WHEN THEY RAISE HER IN THE FOREST?

A. Mary Blair
B. Briar Leah
C. Briar Rose
D. Mary Costa

7 WHAT DO TIANA AND HER FATHER INVITE THE NEIGHBORHOOD TO TASTE?

A. gumbo
B. red beans and rice
C. grits
D. corn bread

8 WHAT IS THE NAME OF MULAN'S DOG?

A. Mushu
B. Little Brother
C. Wanderer
D. Meeko

9 WHAT IS THE NAME OF POCAHONTAS'S BEST FRIEND FROM HER TRIBE?

A. Kocoum
B. Winona
C. Powhatan
D. Nakoma

10 WHAT WAS THE SOURCE OF RAPUNZEL'S MAGICAL POWER?

A. an ancient stone
B. a flower
C. an enchanted feather
D. a dragon's claw

TOP 10 PLACES IN *COCO* WE WANT TO VISIT

10 Santa Cecilia

THERE'S SO MUCH TO EXPLORE IN THE TOWN.

9 The Sunrise Spectacular stadium

8 The tallest building in the Land of the Dead

THE VIEW WOULD BE BREATHTAKING.

7 Plaza de la Cruz

6 Mariachi Plaza

HOW COOL WOULD IT BE TO HEAR ALL THOSE MUSICIANS PERFORM?

5 Rivera family courtyard

4 Marigold Grand Central Station

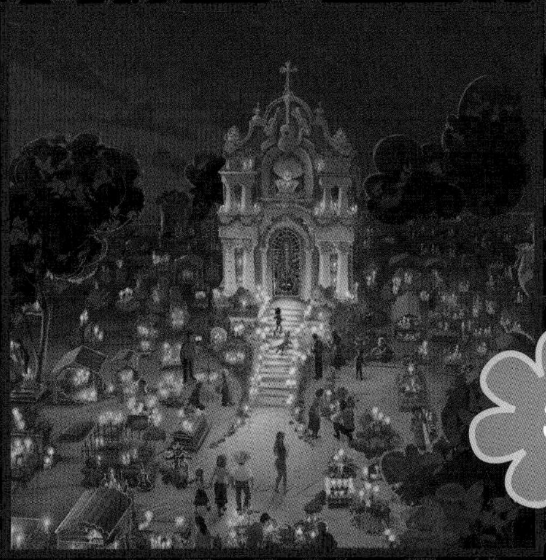

3 Santa Cecilia Cemetery

2 The Marigold Bridge

THERE MUST BE A MILLION PETALS!

1

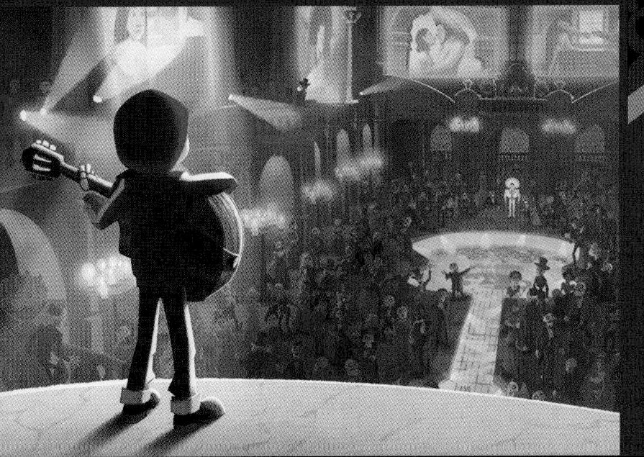

« DE LA CRUZ'S MANSION

THERE'S A POOL SHAPED LIKE A GUITAR!

103

TOP 10 TIMES MIGUEL SPOKE FROM THE HEART

10 "This isn't a dream then. You're all really out there."

TO HIS DEAD ANCESTORS

9 "These aren't just old pictures. They're our family, and they're counting on us to remember them."

MIGUEL IS TEACHING HIS BABY SISTER THE IMPORTANCE OF THE OFRENDA.

8 "My whole life, there's been something that made me different . . . now I know it comes from you."

TO HÉCTOR

7 "I've gotta seize my moment."

6 "Your Papá, he wanted you to have this."

DON'T FORGET HIM, MAMÁ COCO!

 5 "This isn't fair—it's my life! You already had yours."

TO MAMÁ IMELDA

 4 "You don't have to forgive him, but we shouldn't forget him!"

ASKING MAMÁ IMELDA TO HELP HÉCTOR

 3 "You should be the one the world remembers, not de la Cruz!"

TO HÉCTOR

 2 "I don't just want to get de la Cruz's blessing. I need to prove that . . . that I'm worthy of it."

1

"FAMILY COMES FIRST."

TOP 10 REASONS DANTE IS TERRIFIC

10 His version of shake is adorable!

NOT JUST HIS PAW, HIS WHOLE BODY!

9 His tongue is so floppy.

8 He knows how to climb trees.

7 His tiny spirit guide wings are too cute.

6 He finds Miguel and Héctor in the pit.

5

He tries very hard to save Miguel from falling.

4 He tries to bring Miguel back to Héctor.

HE KNOWS MIGUEL'S TRUE PATH.

3 He is so happy rolling in the petals on the Marigold Bridge.

2

He's loyal and persistent.

HE BECOMES AN ALEBRIJE.

FRIDA WAS RIGHT! HE IS A SPIRIT GUIDE.

1

TOP 10 RIVERA FAMILY'S DÍA DE LOS MUERTOS TRADITIONS

 10 Abuelita decorates the ofrenda room with lots and lots of beautiful orange marigolds.

 9 Candles light the way in the dark.

 8 The family decorates with colorful sugar skulls.

THE SKULLS ARE BEAUTIFUL AND MEANINGFUL.

 7 They share stories of their ancestors

 6 The family spends time together.

DID YOU KNOW?

Ofrendas are altars set up on Día de los Muertos to remember and honor ancestors. There is a digital ofrenda in *Coco*'s credits. The photos show people important to the Pixar employees who worked on the film.

5 They enjoy favorite family foods.

ABUELITA'S COOKING LOOKS YUMMY!

4 The children help make a path of petals to guide their ancestors home.

3 The family makes music together.

THAT'S A NEW TRADITION!

2 Papel picado decorates the courtyard.

THE CUT-PAPER PICTURES LOOK SO DELICATE.

1

THEY MAKE AN OFRENDA TO REMEMBER THEIR LOVED ONES.

TOP 10 TIMES *COCO* TOUCHED OUR HEARTS

10 Héctor's picture sinks under the water. **HOW WILL HE BE ON THE OFRENDA?**

9 Héctor, Mamá Imelda, and Mamá Coco cross the Marigold Bridge together.

8 Miguel shows his baby sister the ofrenda.

7 Mamá Imelda changes her mind about Miguel playing music.

^^^^^
DID YOU KNOW?

Pixar animators try very hard to make their art as realistic as possible. But *Coco*'s animators made the skeleton bones less realistic so the characters could show emotion. They can move their eye sockets like eyebrows.

6 Abuelita breaks Miguel's guitar.

AND OUR HEARTS TOO.

5 Héctor talks about missing his little girl.

4 Chicharrón disappears in the final death.

3 Miguel tells Mamá Coco pretty much everything.

LOVE THE WRESTLING MASKS!

2 Miguel and his cousins play music in the family courtyard.

1

MAMÁ COCO'S PICTURE IS ON THE OFRENDA.

SHE WILL BE MISSED AND REMEMBERED.

TOP 10 FAVORITE MUSICAL MOMENTS IN *COCO*

10 Ernesto de la Cruz's final performance in the Land of the Living

TOO BAD ABOUT THAT BELL.

9 Miguel sings at the party to get Ernesto's attention

8 Héctor plays Chicharrón's favorite song

7 Mamá Imelda sings in the Sunrise Spectacular

6 Héctor helps Miguel develop his grito, or loud musical yell

5

Miguel and the whole family sing together

∧∧∧∧∧
DID YOU KNOW?

Whenever anyone plays a guitar in *Coco*, they are playing the notes correctly. Animators filmed real guitarists playing the songs for reference.

4

Miguel suggests some music to add to Frida's performance.

HE'S A COMPOSER *AND* A MUSICIAN.

3

Miguel practices his guitar in his hideout

2

The bands compete in Plaza de la Cruz

SO MANY INCREDIBLE PERFORMANCES!

1

MIGUEL AND MAMÁ COCO SING "REMEMBER ME"

TOP 10 FUNNIEST LINES FROM *COCO*

10 "Watch your step, they make caquitas everywhere."

TÍO FELIPE DOESN'T WANT DIRTY SHOES!

9 "Never name a street dog. They'll follow you forever."

ABUELITA DOESN'T KNOW THAT DANTE ALREADY FOLLOWS MIGUEL EVERYWHERE.

8 "A minute ago I thought I was related to a murderer. You're a total upgrade." —Miguel

7 "Should we tell him there are no restrooms in the Land of the Dead?"—Clerk at the Department of Family Reunions

6 "I'm one Frida short of an opening number."

CECI IS MAD HÉCTOR LOST THE COSTUME.

 5 "Ernesto doesn't *do* rehearsals." —Frida

 4 "I hope you die very soon—you know what I mean." —Ernesto

3 "I thought it might've been one of those made-up things that adults tell kids, like vitamins." —Miguel

2 "Stop pestering the celebrities." —Héctor

 **1** "THAT DEVIL BOX TELLS YOU NOTHING BUT LIES."

MAMÁ IMELDA DOESN'T TRUST COMPUTERS.

TOP 10 FAVORITE FOODS IN *COCO*

10 Mole

9 Chorizo

A SPICY SAUSAGE AND HÉCTOR'S NICKNAME.

8 Pan de muertos

MANY FAMILIES SPEND THE WEEK LEADING UP TO DÍA DE LOS MUERTOS MAKING THIS BREAD.

7 Papaya

IT'S A *HUGE* PART OF FRIDA'S PERFORMANCE.

6 Churros

DID YOU KNOW?

Sugar skulls are decorations made from sugar. Originally, the Aztecs who lived in the area that is modern-day Mexico made these sweets from seeds and honey. Today some are fully edible and some are not.

5 Elotes

YUMMY CORN IN A CHILI-AND-LIME SAUCE WITH CHEESE!

4 Pan dulce

A TASTY SWEET BREAD.

3 Tamales

ALWAYS ACCEPT MORE TAMALES FROM ABUELITA.

2 Taquitos

A PORCUPINE ALEBRIJE MAKES A GREAT SNACK HOLDER.

1

SUGAR SKULLS

TOP 10 REASONS MIGUEL'S HIDEOUT IS AWESOME

10 The rug makes it cozy.

9 There is a fan to keep it cool.

8 He can listen to his favorite songs on a record player.

PERFECT FOR A YOUNG MUSICIAN!

7 There are many musical instruments.

6 It has cool mood lighting.

LOTS OF CANDLES!

5 There's a secret entrance.

4 He can watch the best of Ernesto de la Cruz on videotape.

HE'S MEMORIZED ALL OF ERNESTO'S LINES.

3 Dante and Miguel have a place to hang out together.

2 It's a special place for Miguel's treasures and collectibles.

HE HAS QUITE THE COLLECTION!

1

MIGUEL CAN PRACTICE PLAYING HIS GUITAR.

HE'S PROBABLY SPENT HOURS AND HOURS HERE.

TOP 10
JAW-DROPPING
MOMENTS IN *COCO*

10 When Abuelita throws her sandal

SHE MEANS BUSINESS.

9 Seeing the Día de los Muertos party at Ernesto de la Cruz's mansion

8 When Héctor plays the guitar for Chicharrón

HE'S SO TALENTED!

7 When Miguel becomes invisible to the living

6 When Miguel and Héctor realize they are family

5 Miguel discovers the guitar in Mamá Coco's picture

4 Whenever Pepita does anything

SHE'S INCREDIBLE.

3 When Héctor realizes that Ernesto poisoned him

2 The first time Miguel sees the Marigold Bridge and the Land of the Dead

1

WHEN MIGUEL STRUMS THE GUITAR IN ERNESTO'S TOMB

WOW! WHAT A MOMENT.

TOP 10 REASONS ALEBRIJES ARE FANTASTIC

10 They are magical works of art.

9 They look ordinary in the Land of the Living.

8 Some are good trackers.

←⌐ PEPITA MADE MIGUEL'S FOOTSTEPS GLOW.

7 They are loyal.

6 Some breathe fire.

5 They glow in the dark.

BEST NIGHT-LIGHT EVER!

4 They travel between the Land of the Living and the Land of the Dead.

3 They can be a mix of different animals and creatures.

LIKE THE FROBBIT!

2 They help people find their path.

1

THEY ARE COLORFUL.

VERY, VERY COLORFUL!

QUIZ BREAK!

Are you a *Coco* expert?
Take this quiz and find out!

1 WHERE DO PEOPLE IN THE LAND OF THE DEAD GO WHEN THEY HAVE TROUBLE CROSSING THE BRIDGE?

A Department of Family Reunions
B Family Fun Department
C Department of Ofrendas
D Problem Department

2 WHAT IS THE SHAPE OF ERNESTO'S POOL?

A a guitar
B a skull
C an oval
D a music note

3 WHAT IS MIGUEL'S SHOE SIZE?

A 8.5
B 8
C 7.5
D 7

4 WHICH OF THESE THINGS IS SHAPED LIKE A SKULL IN THE LAND OF THE DEAD?

A a pay phone
B a skull scanner panel
C De la Cruz's fireworks
D all of the above

5

IN REAL LIFE, FRIDA KAHLO IS A FAMOUS _____?

A actress
B singer
C painter
D chef

6

WHO HAS A PICTURE OF JUAN ORTODONCIA ON THE OFRENDA?

A his teacher
B his dentist
C his best friend
D his neighbor

7

WHERE CAN YOU SEE BUZZ AND WOODY IN *COCO*?

A in a piñata stand
B in an alebrije stand
C on a poster in Mariachi Plaza
D on a sugar skull stand

8

MAMÁ IMELDA IS MIGUEL'S _____?

A mother
B grandmother
C great-grandmother
D great-great-grandmother

9

WHAT DOES "UN POCO LOCO" MEAN?

A a poky train
B a little crazy
C a prime location
D a lost pocket

10

WHICH SPIRIT GUIDE HAS A FROG BODY AND RABBIT EARS?

A hoppy
B ribbit
C rabbog
D frobbit

TOP 10 THINGS EVERY RACE CAR NEEDS

10 A cool paint job so you stand out from the other racers

9 The right kind of fuel

BECAUSE YOU HAVE A NEED FOR SPEED!

8 A corporate sponsor

THANKS, RUST-EZE AND DINOCO!

7 A worthy opponent

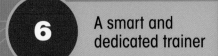

6 A smart and dedicated trainer

^ ^ ^ ^ ^
DID YOU KNOW?
It takes a lot of people who understand science, technology, engineering, and math to design a race car. It has lots of parts that need to work together and at top speed too!

5 A top-notch, fast-as-lightning pit crew

4

A tough, wise crew chief

EVEN THE BEST RACER CAN'T DO IT ALONE.

3 A place to race

A DIRT TRACK, A GRAND PRIX TRACK THROUGH CITY STREETS, A SANDY BEACH, OR EVEN A DRIVING SIMULATOR WILL DO!

2 Focus

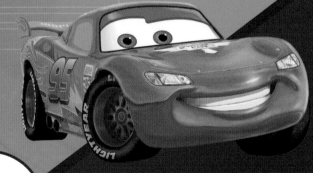

1

CONFIDENCE. "I'M FASTER THAN FAST. QUICKER THAN QUICK. I AM SPEED!" —LIGHTNING MCQUEEN

MATER'S TOP 10 FUNNIEST LINES

10

"Whoa! Git-R-done!"

9

"It goes down faster than elevators full of Winnebagos."

8

"I'm happier than a tornado in a trailer park!"

7

"Hey, I know this might be a bad time right now, but you owe me $32,000 in legal fees."

LEGAL ADVICE IS NOT CHEAP.

6

"You are not a nice guy! Though seriously, I gotta say you do make a quality mud flap at an affordable price."

A GOOD MUD FLAP IS HARD TO FIND.

^ ^ ^ ^ ^
DID YOU KNOW?

The character of Mater is based on a real person who was nicknamed Mater because he loved to eat tomatoes. Mater's design is based on an old, rusty tow truck the filmmakers found when they were doing research for the first *Cars* movie.

5

"I'm startin' to think he knowed you was gonna crash."

MATER THINKS DOC HUDSON IS PRETTY SMART.

4

"You know what I'd do? . . . I don't know. I got nothin'."

3

"Whatever you do, *do not* eat the free pistachio ice cream."

2

"I'm a precisional instrument of speed and aromatics."

JUST ONE OF THE MANY REASONS TO LOVE MATER.

1

"MY NAME'S MATER . . . LIKE *TUH-MATER*, BUT WITHOUT THE *TUH*."

LIGHTNING'S TOP 10 FRIENDSHIP MOMENTS

10 Lightning and Cruz race on the beach together. **THEY REALLY DO MAKE A GREAT TEAM.**

9 Lightning and a rocket-propelled Mater race together in the Radiator Springs Grand Prix.

8 Lightning still thinks of Doc, even after he's gone. **DOC WAS THE BEST MENTOR AND CREW CHIEF AROUND!**

7 Sally and Lightning go for a drive. **AND SHE SHOWS HIM THAT SPECTACULAR VIEW!**

6 Mater becomes Lightning's biggest cheerleader.

MATER HAS ALL THE FAN LOOT: A FOAM LIGHTNING BOLT, A BIG WIG, AND A RACETRACK HAT.

5 Mater takes Lightning out tractor tipping.

4 Lightning tells Mater to be himself no matter where they are.

BEST FRIENDS LIKE YOU JUST THE WAY YOU ARE.

3 When all of his Radiator Springs friends show up to be Lightning's pit crew against Chick and the King.

2 Lightning helps Mater get a ride in the Dinoco helicopter.

DAD-GUM, THAT'S FUN!

1 MATER CALLS LIGHTNING HIS BEST FRIEND FOR THE FIRST TIME. "I KNOWED I MADE A GOOD CHOICE . . . [IN] MY BEST FRIEND."

TOP 10 THINGS TO SEE AND DO IN RADIATOR SPRINGS

10 Have your picture taken next to the Leaning Tower of Tires at Luigi's Casa Della Tires.

9 Change your colors at Ramone's House of Body Art.

8 See a movie at the Radiator Springs Drive-In Theatre.

WHO WOULDN'T WANT TO SEE TOY CAR STORY OR MONSTER TRUCKS, INC.?

7 Check out the Radiator Springs Racing Museum.

6 Go tractor tipping in the pasture.
WATCH OUT FOR FRANK!

5 Take a drive through Ornament Valley. Or check out the mountains of the Cadillac Range.

4 Stay at the Cozy Cone Motel.
SALLY HAS A ROOM WAITING FOR YOU.

3 Buy a bumper sticker from Lizzie at her Radiator Springs Curios shop.

2 Have a snack at Flo's V8 Cafe.
FLO WILL TAKE GOOD CARE OF YOU!

1

CRUISE DOWN THE MAIN STREET AND ENJOY THE NEON LIGHTS.

TOP 10 WAYS TO GET LIGHTNING MCQUEEN TO LOSE HIS COOL

10 Stop timing him on the beach to protect a little crab in the sand.

OH, BUT CRABS ARE SO CUTE!

9

Accidentally win a demolition derby when you're supposed to be helping him train for a race.

JUST STAY AWAY FROM MISS FRITTER!

8 Tell him he's too old to keep racing.

7

Beat him in a race.

HE HATES THAT. JUST ASK JACKSON STORM.

6 Make him pull a paving machine to put asphalt on a road.

5 Make him scrape asphalt off a road when he puts it on wrong.

4 Tell him to turn right to go left without explaining what that means.

THANKS, DOC. VERY HELPFUL.

3 Insult his racing skills.

2 Keep him from getting to the racetrack on time.

1

FORCE HIM TO RETIRE BEFORE HE'S READY.

HE DECIDES WHEN HE'S DONE RACING.

TOP 10 HIGH-OCTANE RACES

10

The race through London. Good thing Holley Shiftwell installed those rocket boosters on Mater!

9 The race through Italy

KEEP AN EYE OUT FOR LEMONS!

8 The race through Japan. Mater with a headset turns out not to be such a great idea.

7 The race when a young Doc Hudson has a terrible crash

6 The tiebreaking "Race of the Century" with Lightning McQueen, Chick Hicks, and the King

"BOOGITY, BOOGITY, BOOGITY!" —DARRELL CARTRIP

5 The Crazy 8 race at Thunder Hollow

4

When Lightning McQueen races Jackson Storm on the simulator—and crashes through the screen.

⌐»

3 The Florida 500 race at the Florida International Super Speedway

CRUZ FINALLY REALIZES HER DREAM.

2 The Piston Cup three-way tie between Lightning McQueen, Chick Hicks, and the King

1

DOC AND LIGHTNING MCQUEEN'S EPIC RACE AROUND WILLY'S BUTTE

TOP 10 QUOTES FROM CARS FRIENDS

10

"You can use anything negative as fuel to push through to the positive." —Cruz

9 "You got a lotta stuff, kid." —Doc

8 "You are a racer. Use that."

LIGHTNING GIVES CRUZ THE CONFIDENCE SHE NEEDS IN HER FIRST RACE.

7 "Hud saw something in you that you didn't even see in yourself." —Smokey

6

"I've wanted to become a racer forever. Because of you." —Cruz

5

"Lightning wins. He decides when he's done racing. That was the deal. Hi, I'm his lawyer."

SALLY TAKING CARE OF BUSINESS.

4

"The racing *is* the reward. Not the stuff!" —Lightning

3

"Life's too short to take no for an answer." —Louise

2

"Racing wasn't the best part of Hud's life. You were."

SMOKEY TELLING LIGHTNING HOW DOC REALLY FELT.

1

"DON'T FEAR FAILURE. BE AFRAID OF NOT HAVING THE CHANCE. YOU HAVE THE CHANCE." —SALLY

TOP 10 QUOTES FROM TROUBLEMAKERS AND BAD GUYS

10 "MOOOOO!"

UH-OH! HERE COMES FRANK!

9 "We got ourselves a *nodder.*" —Boost

8 "Hey, McQueen, that must be really embarrassing. But I wouldn't worry about it . . . because I didn't do it! Ha Ha Ha!" —Chick Hicks

7 "I'm about to commit a movin' violation!" —Miss Fritter

6 "You have no idea what a pleasure it is for me to finally beat you."

YES, JACKSON STORM SAID BEAT.

5 "The next time he makes a stop, instead of saying 'ka-chow,' he's gonna go 'ka-boom!'"

ACER THINKS HE'S SO CLEVER.

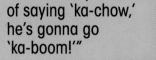

4 "No! You DON'T belong on this track!" Jackson Storm wants Cruz out of the way—and out of the race.

3 "You actually care about that race car. A pity you didn't warn him in time." —Professor Zündapp

2 "You're insane, you are! Deactivate!"

MILES AXLEROD HAS TO STOP HIS OWN EVIL PLAN.

1

"HEY, LIGHTNING! YO! MCQUEEN! SERIOUSLY, THAT WAS SOME PRETTY DARN NICE RACIN' OUT THERE. BY ME!"
—CHICK HICKS

TOP 10
EDGE-OF-YOUR-SEAT
SCENES

10 Mater and Lightning McQueen get chased by Frank after tractor tipping.

9 Lightning McQueen flips out of control in the last race of the season.

8 Mater escapes from the secret lemon summit meeting.

THAT WAS A CLOSE CALL!

7 Smokey and the Legends take Lightning and Cruz into the woods to race in the dark.

6 Chick Hicks causes the King to crash.

THAT'S NO WAY TO WIN.

5 Mater, Finn McMissile, and Holley Shiftwell get trapped inside Big Bentley.

DAD-GUM! DAD-GUM! DAD-GUM!

4 Cruz and Lightning McQueen try to survive the Crazy 8 race.

3 When the bomb attached to Mater ticks down to its final seconds.

2 When Cruz flips over Jackson Storm to win the race.

SHE REALLY IS A RACER!

1 LIGHTNING MCQUEEN RACES JACKSON STORM, LOSES CONTROL, AND CRASHES. OUCH! THAT HAD TO HURT—IN MORE WAYS THAN ONE.

TOP 10 CARS FUN FACTS

10 The characters' license plates have hidden meanings.

FOR EXAMPLE, DOC IS A 1951 HUDSON HORNET AND A MEDICAL DOCTOR, SO HIS PLATES SAY 51HHMD.

9 Animators made more than forty-three thousand sketches of cars for the first *Cars* movie.

8 The jet tails in the movies' sky scenes are actually tire tracks!

7 Flo's V8 Cafe looks like the V-shaped parts of a car engine.

ONE ORDER OF OIL, COMING RIGHT UP!

6

The rocky hills around Radiator Springs are shaped like old car parts.

5

Lightning McQueen's 95 stands for 1995, the year *Toy Story* was made.

LIGHTNING AND MATER, WOODY AND BUZZ—FANTASTIC FRIENDS, AWESOME ADVENTURES!

4

Life-size, remote-control versions of Lightning McQueen, Mater, Finn McMissile, Cruz Ramirez, and Jackson Storm were used to advertise the Cars movies.

3

Mater is the only Cars character with crooked teeth.

2

The Piston Cup trophy is shaped like an engine piston with wings attached.

PISTONS HELP A CAR'S ENGINE GO, GO, GO!

1

THE IDEA FOR *CARS* CAME FROM AN OLD CARTOON ABOUT A LITTLE BLUE CAR.

TOP 10 WINNING TIPS FROM DOC HUDSON

10

"You look! All I see is a bunch of empty cups."

YOU RACE BECAUSE YOU LOVE IT, NOT FOR TROPHIES!

9

"You give it too much throttle, and you're in the tulips."

STAY OUTTA THOSE TULIPS.

8

"Ha, that ain't racing. That wasn't even a Sunday drive. That was one lap. Racing is five hundred of those."

7

"Find a groove that works for you and get that lap back."

6

"If I were you, I'd quit yappin' and start workin'."

ALWAYS GOOD ADVICE!

5

"I knew you needed a crew chief, but I didn't know it was this bad."

EVERYBODY NEEDS A LITTLE HELP SOMETIMES.

4

"All right, if you can drive as good as you can fix a road, then you can win this race with your eyes shut. Now get back out there."

YOU CAN'T WIN A RACE IF YOU'RE NOT ON THE RACETRACK!

3

"When is the last time you cared about something except yourself, hot rod?"

2

"I didn't come all this way to see you quit."

1

"IF YOU'RE GOIN' HARD ENOUGH LEFT, YOU'LL FIND YOURSELF TURNIN' RIGHT."

LEARN HOW TO DO WHAT YOU NEED TO DO TO GET WHERE YOU WANT TO BE.

QUIZ BREAK!

Can you cross the finish line with winning answers for this Cars quiz?

1

WHAT IS THE NAME OF LIGHTNING MCQUEEN'S TRANSPORT TRUCK?

A Minny
B Mack
C Mater
D Macaroni

2

WHAT COLOR WAS MATER BEFORE HE TURNED RUSTY?

A Red
B Yellow
C Light blue
D Purple

3

WHO WINS THE PISTON CUP BY HITTING ANOTHER RACER?

A Lightning McQueen
B The King
C Doc Hudson
D Chick Hicks

LIGHTNING MCQUEEN'S FAMOUS CATCHPHRASE IS

4

A Ka-chow!
B Woo-hoo!
C Boo-yah!
D Yee-haw!

5

WHICH OF THESE IS NOT THE NAME OF A CARS CHARACTER?

A Chick Hicks
B Ivan
C Smokey
D Andy

6

IN *CARS*, WHAT DOES MATER TAKE A RIDE IN?

A A helicopter
B A train
C A Winnebago
D A transport truck

7

WHAT KIND OF CAR IS DOC HUDSON?

A Hudson Hawk
B Blue Bomber
C Hudson Hornet
D Road Rally Racer

WHO RUNS THE COZY CONE MOTEL?

8

A Flo
B Sally Carrera
C Lizzie
D Luigi

9

WHAT IS CRUZ RAMIREZ'S DREAM JOB?

A Trainer for the best young racers
B Pit crew chief
C Attorney
D Racer

MAKE YOUR OWN DISNEY TOP 10

Now it's time to pick your favorites. Have some changes you'd like to make to one of the lists in this book? Go for it! Or maybe you have your own ideas about the best parts of your favorite movie. Make a new list, such as

- **JACK-JACK'S TOP 10 POWERS**

- **THE TOP 10 BEST THINGS ABOUT BEING A CAR**

- **THE TOP 10 PEOPLE IN YOUR LIFE WORTH MELTING FOR**

Use your imagination to come up with more Top 10 Disney lists!

MY

Disney

TOP 10:

10. _____

9. _____

8. _____

7. _____

6. _____

5. _____

4. _____

3. _____

2. _____

1. _____

Lerner Publications Company
A division of Lerner Publishing Group, Inc.
241 First Avenue North
Minneapolis, MN 55401 USA

For reading levels and more information, look up this title at www.lernerbooks.com.

Main body text set in ITC Avant Garde Gothic 13/14.
Typeface provided by International Typeface Corp.

Library of Congress Cataloging-in-Publication Data

The Cataloging-in-Publication Data for *The Big Book of Disney Top 10s:
    Fun Facts and Cool Trivia* is on file at the Library of Congress.
ISBN 978-1-5415-5266-1 (pbk.)
ISBN 978-1-5415-5267-8 (eb pdf)

Manufactured in the United States of America
1 45651 41664-9/12/2010